HOUGHTON MIFFLIN HARCOURT

JOURNEYS

Program Authors

James F. Baumann · David J. Chard · Jamal Cooks
J. David Cooper · Russell Gersten · Marjorie Lipson
Lesley Mandel Morrow · John J. Pikulski · Héctor H. Rivera
Mabel Rivera · Shane Templeton · Sheila W. Valencia
Catherine Valentino · MaryEllen Vogt

Consulting Author

Irene Fountas

HOUGHTON MIFFLIN HARCOURT
School Publishers

Welcome, Reader!

This year you will read many wonderful stories. In this first book, you will meet lots of pals, a special grandpa, and a curious monkey who gets into trouble. You will read about neighborhood helpers and a cat who takes a ride on a train. Your reading will get stronger each day!

Are you ready to begin your reading journey? Just turn the page!

Sincerely,

The Authors

Around the Neighborhood

Big Idea Everyone can be a good neighbor.

Lesson **2**

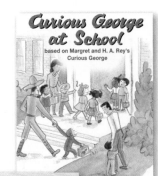

Lucia's Neighborhood

City Mouse and Country Mouse

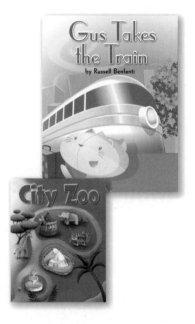

Around the Neighborhood

Unit 1

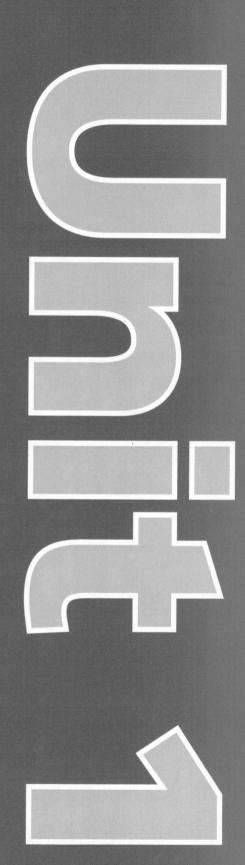

Big Idea

Everyone can be a good neighbor.

Paired Selections

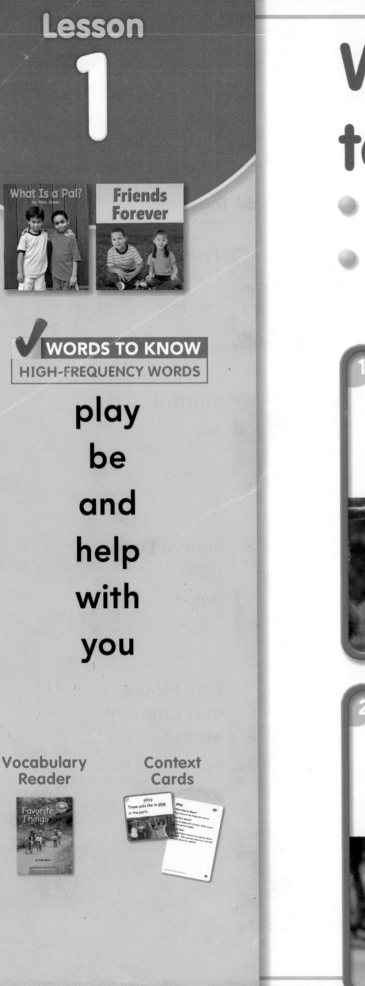

What Is a Pal?
by Nina Crews

Friends Forever

✓ **WORDS TO KNOW**
HIGH-FREQUENCY WORDS

play

be

and

help

with

you

Vocabulary
Reader

Favorite
Things
by Katie Sharp

Context
Cards

Read
Together

Words to Know

● Read each Context Card.

● Make up a sentence that uses a blue word.

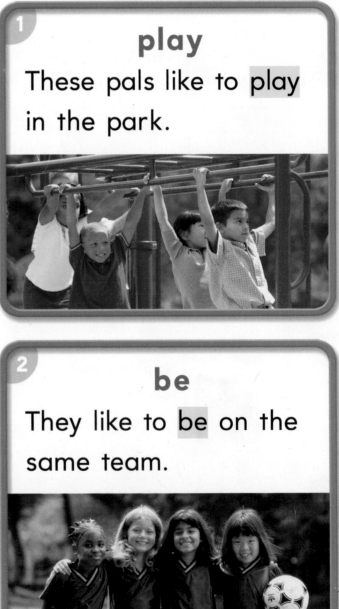

1
play
These pals like to play in the park.

2
be
They like to be on the same team.

3 and
The children share the paper **and** paint.

4 help
These pals **help** each other wash the dog.

5 with
The boy was in a show **with** his pals.

6 you
I like when **you** play this game with me.

Background

✓ **WORDS TO KNOW**   **How to Be a Good Pal**

1. First, you need to find a pal.

2. Smile and say hello.

3. Ask the pal to play.

4. Take turns with your pal.

5. Be kind.

6. Help your pal.

Who Can Be a Pal?

pet

boy

girl

mom

dad

Comprehension

Read Together

TARGET SKILL Main Idea

Most nonfiction selections have one **topic**. The topic is the one big idea that the selection is about. The **main idea** is the most important idea about the topic. **Details** are facts that tell more about the main idea.

As you read **What Is a Pal?,** think about the topic and main idea. Tell about them in your own words. Fill in a web.

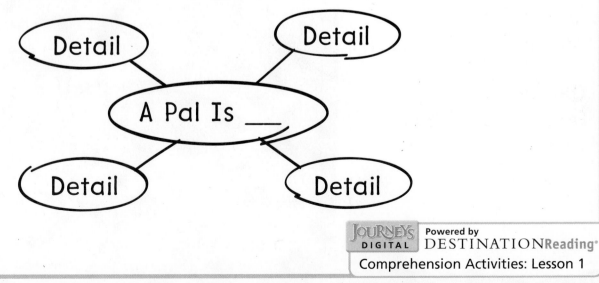

What Is a Pal?
by Nina Crews

✔ **WORDS TO KNOW**

play	help
be	with
and	you

✔ **TARGET SKILL**

Main Idea Tell the important idea about a topic.

✔ **TARGET STRATEGY**

Summarize Stop to tell important ideas as you read.

GENRE
Informational text gives facts about a topic.

Meet the Author and Photographer

Nina Crews

Nina Crews comes from a very creative family. Her parents, Donald Crews and Ann Jonas, are both well-known artists. For her own artwork, Ms. Crews likes to make collages out of photos.

What Is a Pal?

written and photographed by Nina Crews

Essential Question

What is important about being a friend?

A pal can help you.

Sam and Nat can help Dan.

A pal can play with you.

Tad, Cam, and Nan can play.

A pal can be a pet.

A pal can be Dad.

A pal can be with you.

A pal is fun to be with!

Are you a pal?

My Pal

Draw a Pal Draw a picture of a pal. Why is he or she a good pal? Write about your picture.

PERSONAL RESPONSE

Turn and Talk — **Answer a Question**

Read the last page of the selection with a partner. Then answer the question. Talk about how you are a pal to others.

MAIN IDEA

Friends Forever

Connect to Poetry

play	help
be	with
and	you

GENRE
Poetry uses the sounds of words to show pictures and feelings.

TEXT FOCUS
Rhyme is words with the same ending sound, like blue and two. Clap when you hear words that rhyme at the end of lines.

Friends Forever

How can you be a good friend?
You can play with your friends.
You can share with friends and
help them.

Damon & Blue

Damon & Blue
Just us two
Cruising up the avenue.

You strut, you glide
But mark our stride
Can't beat us when we're
side by side.

by Nikki Grimes

Wait for Me

Wait for me
and I'll be there
and we'll walk home together,
if it's raining
puddle pails
or if it's sunny weather.

Wait for me
and I'll be there
and we'll walk home together.
You wear red
and I'll wear blue,
and we'll be friends forever.

by Sarah Wilson

Jambo

Jambo Jambo
ambo ambo
mbo mbo
bo bo bo
o o o
bo bo bo
mbo mbo
ambo ambo
Jambo Jambo
HI! HELLO!
Did you Did you
did you know
Jambo means
hello hello!

*by Sundaira
Morninghouse*

Respond to Poetry
- Listen to the poems again. Join in!
- Say more rhyming lines that could be added to one of the poems.

Making Connections

Read Together

Text to Self

Write Sentences Write sentences to tell your classmates about favorite things you do with your pals.

Text to Text

Discuss Characters How are the friends in the poems like the pals in the story?

Text to World

Connect to Social Studies Can neighbors be pals? What are some things that good neighbors do?

Grammar

Read Together

Nouns Some words name people. Some words name animals. Words that name people and animals are called **nouns**.

Nouns for People

boy

dad

sister

baby

Nouns for Animals

dog

cat

pig

cow

Talk about each picture with a partner. Name the nouns you see. Then write a noun from the box to name each picture. Use another sheet of paper.

man   bird   girl   fish   mom

1.

2.

3.

4.

5.

Grammar in Writing

Share your writing with a partner. Talk about the nouns you used.

Writing About Us

☑ **Ideas** Dan drew and wrote about his pals.
Then he thought about what details to add.
He added a picture of a ball and a **label**.

Revised Paper

my pal Max

soccer ball

Writing Traits Checklist

☑ **Ideas** Does my paper have interesting details about my pals?

☑ Did I use nouns in my labels?

☑ Did I write letters neatly and correctly?

What do the details in Dan's paper tell you about his pals? Now revise your own writing. Use the Checklist.

Final Paper

My Pals

my mom

van

my brother

computer

my pal Max

soccer ball

Star

rabbit

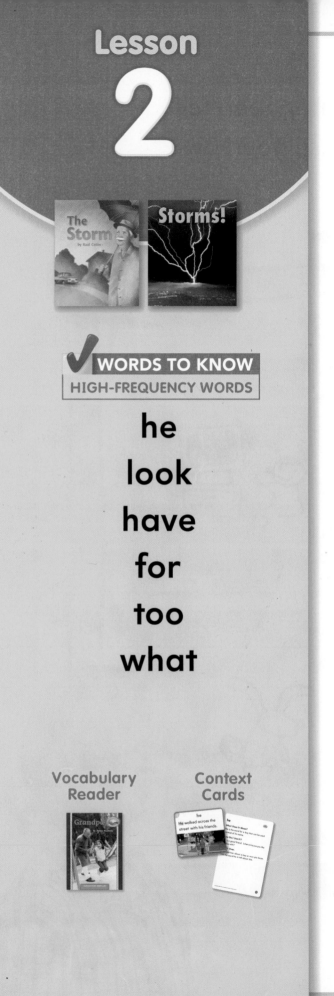

✓ **WORDS TO KNOW**
HIGH-FREQUENCY WORDS

he

look

have

for

too

what

Vocabulary
Reader

Context
Cards

Words to Know

● Read each Context Card.

● Choose two blue words.
Use them in sentences.

1

he

He walked across the
street with his friends.

2

look

Children look at water
from the fire hose.

3. have

Firefighters **have** fast trucks to get to a fire.

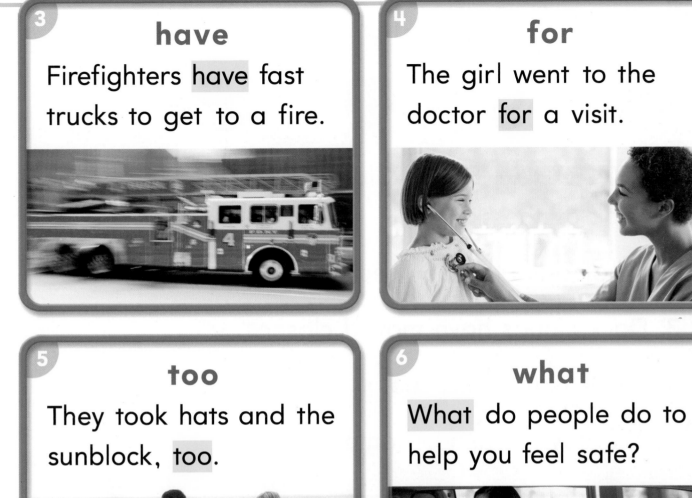

4. for

The girl went to the doctor **for** a visit.

5. too

They took hats and the sunblock, **too**.

6. what

What do people do to help you feel safe?

Background

✔ **WORDS TO KNOW** **Storm Clouds**

1. **Look** at the sky!

2. **What** does the boy see?

3. Dark clouds **have** moved closer.

4. There is thunder, **too**.

5. The boy heads **for** home.

6. **He** wants to stay dry!

How do you know a storm is coming?
What do you see and hear in a storm?

Comprehension

✔ **TARGET SKILL** Understanding Characters

Characters are the people and animals in a story. When you read, think about what the characters say and do. Good readers use these clues to figure out how characters feel and why they do the things they do.

Read **The Storm**. Use the words and pictures to figure out what Pop says and does to help Tim.

Speaking	Acting

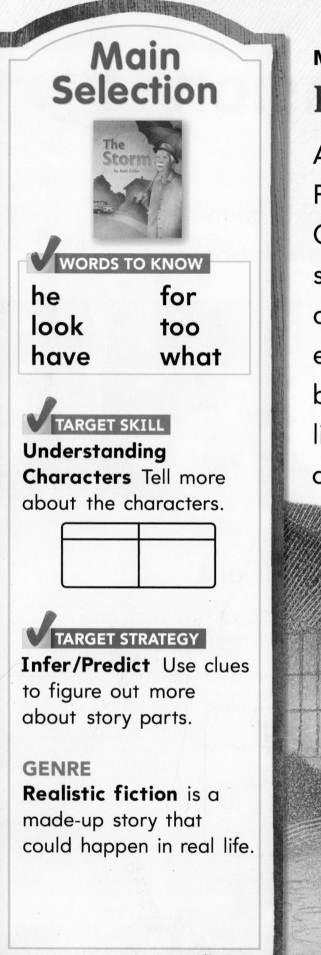

✔ **WORDS TO KNOW**

he	for
look	too
have	what

✔ **TARGET SKILL**

Understanding Characters Tell more about the characters.

✔ **TARGET STRATEGY**

Infer/Predict Use clues to figure out more about story parts.

GENRE

Realistic fiction is a made-up story that could happen in real life.

Meet the Author and Illustrator

Raúl Colón

As a little boy in Puerto Rico, Raúl Colón was often very sick. He spent a lot of time inside, drawing. He even made his own comic books. Today Mr. Colón lives in New York and works as an artist and a writer.

The Storm

written and illustrated
by Raúl Colón

Essential Question

What clues tell you how a character feels?

Pop has come in.
Look! He is wet.

Tim and Rip ran to him.

Tim, Rip, and Pop have fun.

Tim had to go to bed.

What did Tim and Rip see?

Tim hid in his bed!
Rip hid, too!

Look what Pop had for Tim.
Tim had a sip.

Pop had a hug for Tim.
He had a hug for Rip, too.

Pop sat with Tim and Rip.

Your Turn

A Dark and Stormy Night

Act It Out Act out the story with a partner. Decide who will play Tim and who will play Pop. Use words and actions to show how Tim and Pop feel. PARTNERS

Turn and Talk — Tim's Feelings

Look at page 45 with a partner. Talk about how Tim feels and why he feels that way. Use the picture and the words on the page to help you.

UNDERSTANDING CHARACTERS

49

Connect to Science

GENRE

Informational text gives facts on a topic. Find storm facts. This is from a science textbook.

TEXT FOCUS

Photographs show true pictures with important details. Use these photographs to find out information about storms.

Storms!

A storm is a strong wind with rain or snow. It may have hail or sleet. Warm, light air goes up quickly. It mixes with high, cold air. Look! It's a storm.

This is a lightning storm in Pampa, Texas.

Kinds of Storms

A thunderstorm has thunder and lightning. It can bring heavy rain.

A tornado is a strong, twisting wind. It is shaped like a cone.

A hurricane is a very big storm. It has strong, spinning winds and rain.

A dust storm is a strong wind that carries dust for miles.

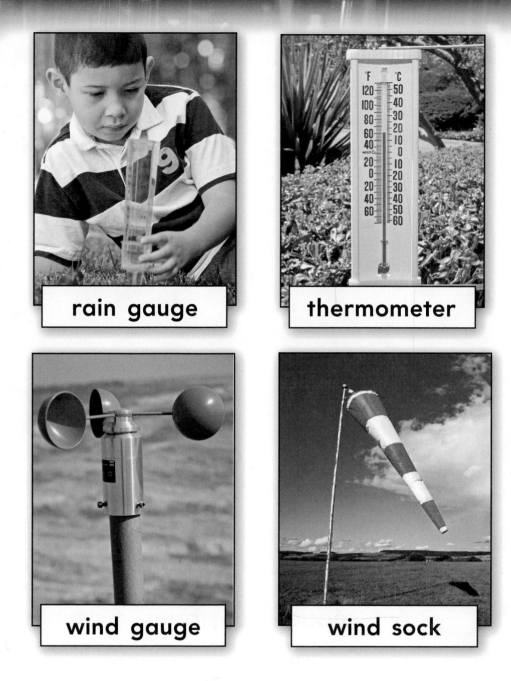

rain gauge

thermometer

wind gauge

wind sock

Measuring Storms

A scientist has tools for measuring storms. He measures heat and cold. He measures the wind. He measures rainfall and snowfall, too.

What storms have you seen?

Making Connections

Read Together

Text to Self

Write Sentences Write about a time you saw a storm. How did the weather change?

Text to Text

Retell and Describe With a small group, talk about storms you have learned about. Decide what kind of storm Tim and Rip saw. Listen to each other.

Text to World

Connect to Social Studies How can neighbors help each other in a storm? Draw a picture.

Grammar

Nouns Some words name places. Some words name things. Words that name places and things are called **nouns**.

Nouns for Places

house

sky

road

garden

pond

Nouns for Things

book

bed

chair

door

rug

Talk about each picture with a partner. Name the nouns you see. Then write a noun from the box to name each picture. Use another sheet of paper.

| milk | coat | room | city | clock |

1.

2.

3.

4.

5.

Grammar in Writing

Share your writing. Talk about the nouns you used.

Writing About Us

☑ **Ideas** Kit drew and wrote about her family trip to the beach. Then she thought of new details. She added a **caption** to explain her picture.

Revised Paper

We saw a fish.

Writing Traits Checklist

☑ **Ideas** Does my paper have interesting details about my family trip?

☑ Do my captions explain the pictures?

☑ Did I use nouns to name places or things?

56

Look for nouns in Kit's final paper. Then revise your own writing. Use the Checklist.

Final Paper

Our Trip to the Beach

my family

a castle we made

We saw a fish.

We found shells.

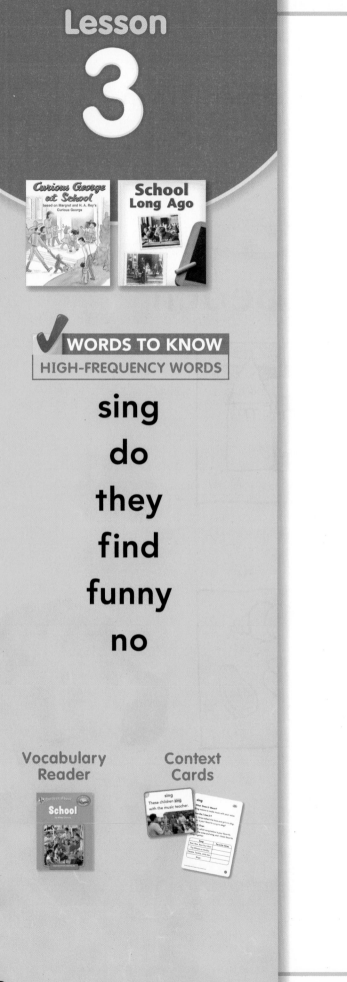

✔ **WORDS TO KNOW**
HIGH-FREQUENCY WORDS

sing

do

they

find

funny

no

Vocabulary
Reader

Context
Cards

Words to Know

● Read each Context Card.

● Ask a question that uses one of the blue words.

1
sing
These children sing with the music teacher.

2
do
The school principal has many things to do.

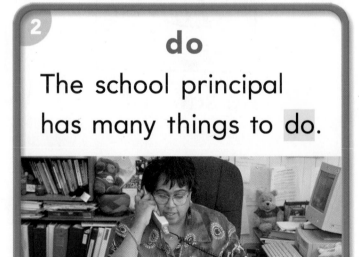

3 **they**

They like to work together in class.

4 **find**

The librarian helps children find books.

5 **funny**

The art teacher drew a funny animal.

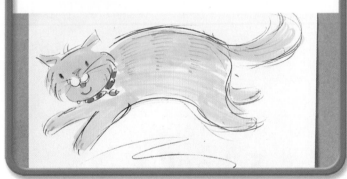

6 **no**

It is safe to cross when no cars are coming.

Background

Read Together

✔ WORDS TO KNOW **One School Day**

1. Children do a lot at school.

2. They read books.

3. They find out many things!

4. They sing songs.

5. They draw funny pictures.

6. Are they done?
   No, they do lots more!

art materials

Things To Do at School

| read books | eat lunch | learn math | sing songs |

Comprehension

✓ **TARGET SKILL** Sequence of Events

Many stories tell about events in the order in which they happen. This order is called the **sequence of events.** The sequence of events is what happens **first**, **next**, and **last** in a story.

First   **Next**   **Last**

As you read **Curious George at School**, think about what happens first, next, and last.

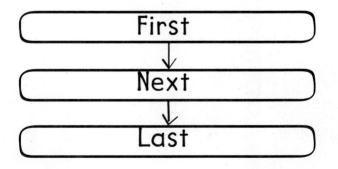

First

↓

Next

↓

Last

JOURNEYS DIGITAL **Powered by** DESTINATIONReading®
Comprehension Activities: Lesson 3

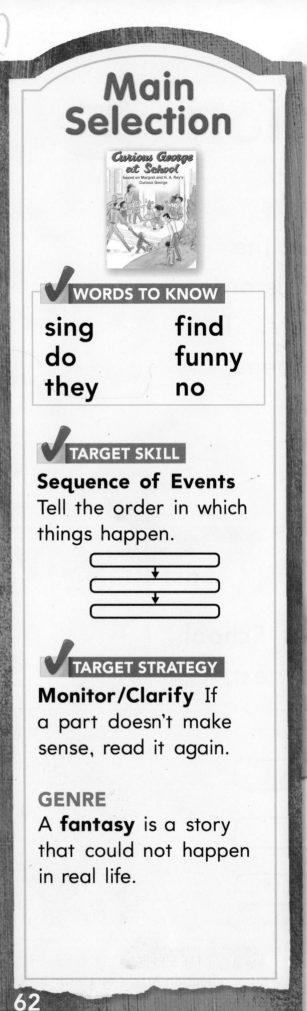

Meet the Creators

Margret and H. A. Rey

Children all over the
world love Curious George!
The Reys' books have been
published in Spanish, French,
Swedish, Japanese, and many
other languages. Since the
Reys wrote their first book
about the curious little
monkey, George has starred
in more than 40 books, a TV
show, and a movie.

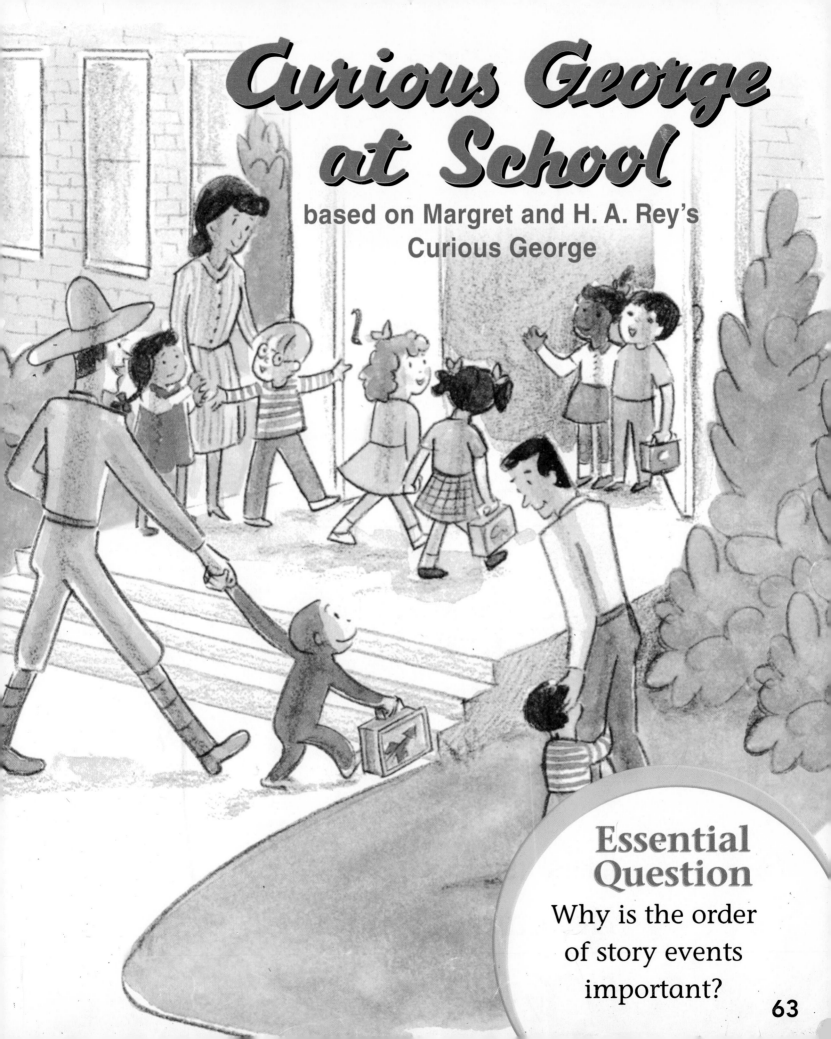

Curious George at School

based on Margret and H. A. Rey's
Curious George

Essential Question

Why is the order
of story events
important?

This is George.
He can help a lot.

George can sing.
He is funny.

He can see the paints.

Mix, mix, mix a bit.
Mix, mix, mix a lot!

It is a big mess!

George ran.
What did he find?

He got a mop.
He had a big job to do.

No, no!
It is a big, BIG mess!
George is sad, sad, sad.

Kids help him do a big job.
They can help him a lot.
He is not sad!

First Day of School

Write a Sentence

George does a lot on his first day of school. What did you do on your first day? Draw a picture of one thing you did. Write a sentence about it.

PERSONAL RESPONSE

Turn and Talk — A Big Mess

What happens after George sees the paints? Talk about it with a partner. Be sure to tell the events in order. Then tell what might happen next in the story.

SEQUENCE OF EVENTS

School
Long Ago

Connect to Social Studies

✔ **WORDS TO KNOW**

sing	find
do	funny
they	no

GENRE

Informational text gives facts about a topic. This is from a social studies textbook. Read to find out what the topic is.

TEXT FOCUS

A **chart** is a drawing that lists information in a clear way. What can you learn from the chart on page 76?

School Long Ago

How did children get to school? Was going to school long ago different from going to school today? Let's find out! There were no school buses long ago. Some children had to walk far to get to school.

What did children bring to school?
Long ago, children did not have
backpacks. They carried their
things for school in their arms.
Children did not have a lot
of paper long ago. They
used chalk to write on small
boards called slates.

What did children learn?

Long ago, children learned reading, writing, and math. Some teachers taught children funny songs to sing. What do children learn in school today?

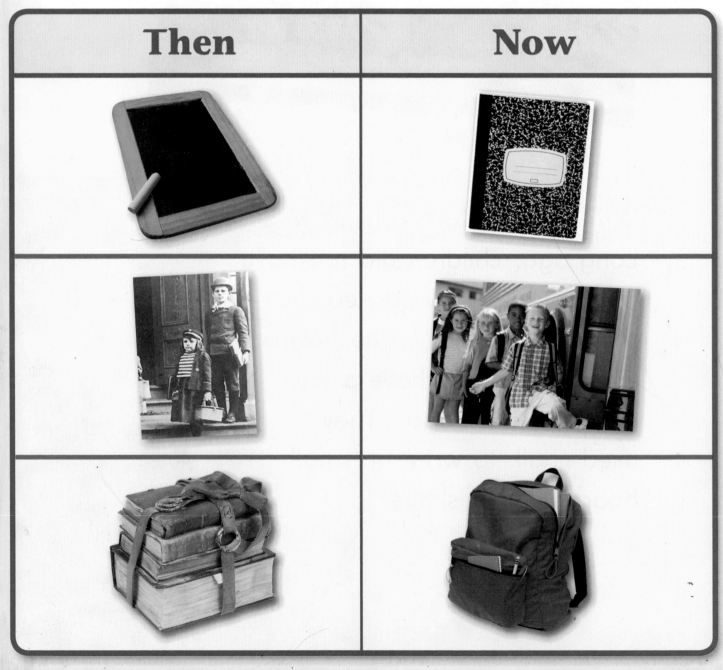

Then	Now

Making Connections

Read Together

Curious George at School — based on Margret and H. A. Rey's Curious George

School Long Ago

Text to Self

Connect to Experiences Think of something Curious George did that you have also done. Write about it.

Text to Text

Compare Stories Is the story about Curious George true or make-believe? How do you know? Tell how you know **School Long Ago** is a true story.

Text to World

Draw a Map Draw a map of your classroom. Show where you sit.

Grammar

Read Together

Action Verbs Some words tell what people and animals do. These action words are called **verbs**.

hop

play

jog

hit

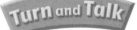

Write a verb from the box to name the action in each picture. Use another sheet of paper. Then act out one of the verbs. Have a partner guess the verb.

| paint | help | sip | mix |

1.

2.

3.

4.

Grammar in Writing

When you revise your writing, use action verbs to tell about things you do.

Writing About Us

☑ **Word Choice** Writers use exact nouns to help give readers a clear picture.

Leah wrote about school activities. Later, she changed **things** to a noun that is exact.

Revised Draft

books
We all read ~~things~~.
∧

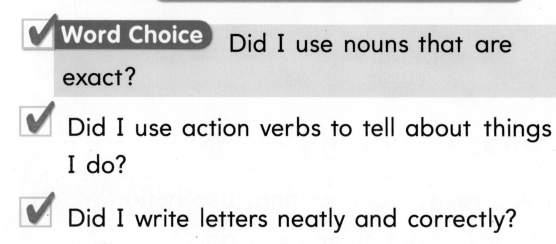

Writing Traits Checklist

☑ **Word Choice** Did I use nouns that are exact?

☑ Did I use action verbs to tell about things I do?

☑ Did I write letters neatly and correctly?

Find nouns and verbs in Leah's final copy.
Then revise your writing. Use the Checklist.

Fun at School

We all read books.

I write stories.

Ani feeds our mice.

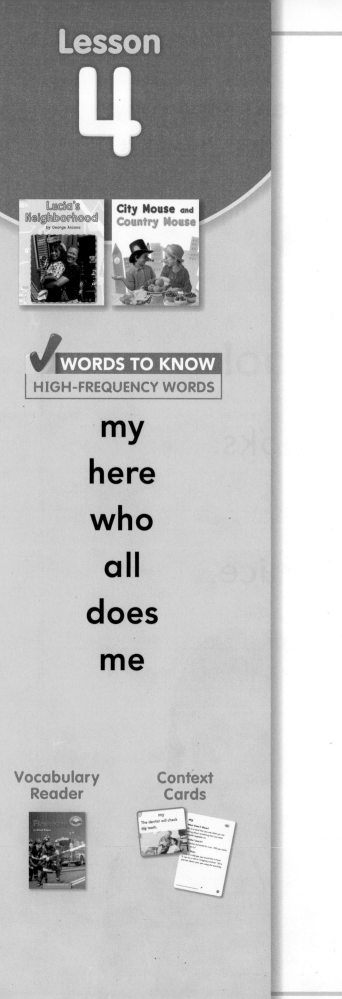

✓ **WORDS TO KNOW**
HIGH-FREQUENCY WORDS

my

here

who

all

does

me

Vocabulary Reader

Context Cards

Words to Know

● Read each Context Card.

● Tell about a picture, using the blue word.

1

my

The dentist will check my teeth.

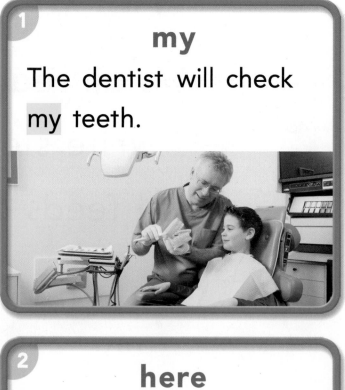

2

here

The firefighters keep their trucks here.

3
who
Who brings the mail to your house?

4
all
The baker made all of these rolls.

5
does
Does this vet take care of dogs?

6
me
The zookeeper let me pet the koala.

Background Read Together

✓ **WORDS TO KNOW** **Good Neighbors**

1. Come to my neighborhood!

2. People are friendly here.

3. We all help each other.

4. How does my neighbor help?

5. She helps me plant the garden.

6. Who will I help today?

How has someone helped you?
How can you help someone?

Comprehension

✓ **TARGET SKILL** Text and Graphic Features

Authors may use **special features** to tell about the topic of a selection. Labels and captions give information about photos. Photos, graphs, maps, and drawings help explain a topic. Good readers think about special features to understand what the author wants them to know.

As you read **Lucia's Neighborhood**, think about the special features. Use a chart like this one to tell what the author wants you to know.

Feature	Purpose

Main Selection

Lucia's Neighborhood
by George Ancona

✔ WORDS TO KNOW

my	all
here	does
who	me

✔ TARGET SKILL

Text and Graphic Features Tell how words go with photos.

✔ TARGET STRATEGY

Question Ask questions about what you read.

GENRE

Informational text gives facts about a topic. Find facts as you read this selection.

86

Meet the Author and Photographer

George Ancona

What do you like to do for fun? George Ancona enjoys dancing, listening to salsa music, and spending time with his grandchildren. He does not like to watch TV or send e-mail. Mr. Ancona has written many books, including **Mi Música/My Music.**

35

Lucia's Neighborhood

written and photographed by George Ancona

Essential Question

What information do words and pictures give?

Hi! I am Lucia.
Can I get a goal?

Yes! We win.
We all get pins.

Bakery

What can Mom and I do?
Look what we get here.

I can look at pets here.
It is fun.

Mom let me get a plant here.
It is not big yet.

Who can fix the street?
Here is the man who can fix it.

Garage

Who can fix a car?
Here is the man who can fix it.

Who has on firefighter's pants?
They are too big to fit me yet!

Does the librarian help me?
Yes!

We sit and look at my book.

My Home

Is it fun to be home?
You bet it is!

Lucia's Neighborhood

Make a Map Draw a map that shows places Lucia likes to visit in her neighborhood. Label your map with the names of the places. SOCIAL STUDIES

 Turn and Talk — **Words and Pictures**

Choose one place that Lucia visited. Describe the place to a partner. Use the photo and the words on the page to help you.

TEXT AND GRAPHIC FEATURES

City Mouse and Country Mouse

Connect to Traditional Tales

✔ **WORDS TO KNOW**

my	all
here	does
who	me

GENRE

A **fable** is a short story in which a character learns a lesson.

TEXT FOCUS

Many tales begin with **Once upon a time.** Why do you think the storyteller uses these words?

Readers' Theater

City Mouse and Country Mouse

retold by Debbie O'Brien

Cast

Country Mouse

City Mouse

Cat

Once upon a time, there were two mice.

I love my country home. Come eat with me.

I like city food better.

Come with me to the city. We will eat like kings.

 I will come.

 Here is my home.

 Look at all this yummy food!

 Meow, meow. I will have mice for lunch!

 Who is that?

 It's Cat! Run and hide.

 City Mouse, my home does not have fine food, but it is safe. I'm going back to the country.

Making Connections

Read Together

Text to Self

Respond to the Story What lesson does Country Mouse learn? Has anything like this ever happened to you? Write about it.

Text to Text

Connect to Social Studies How do Lucia and the mice feel about their neighbors? How do you know?

Text to World

Discuss Neighborhoods Who or what makes your neighborhood special?

Grammar

Read Together

Adjectives Some words describe people, animals, places, or things. These describing words are called **adjectives**. Adjectives can describe by telling size or shape.

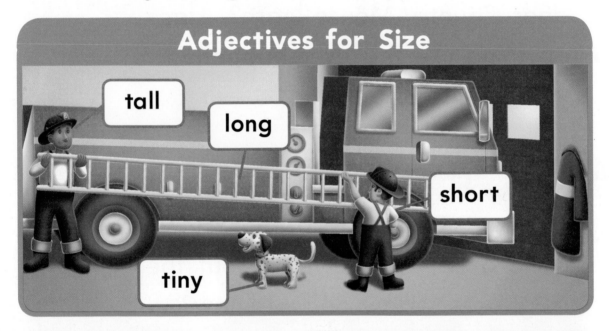

Adjectives for Size

tall

long

short

tiny

Adjectives for Shape

curved

thin

round

oval

flat

Think of an adjective for size or shape to describe each picture. Write the word on another sheet of paper.

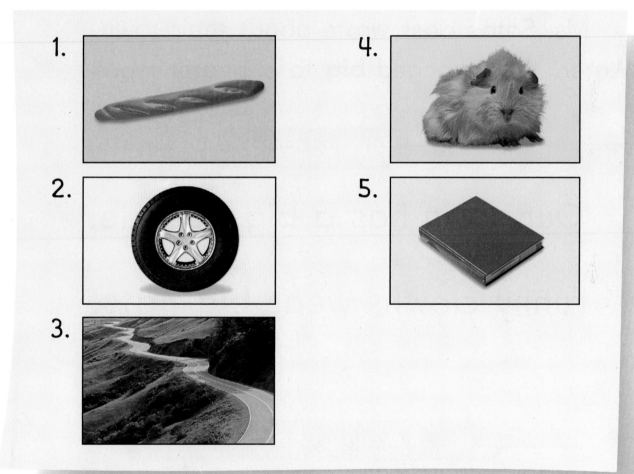

1.

2.

3.

4.

5.

Grammar in Writing

When you revise your class story, look for places where you can add some adjectives.

Writing About Us

Read Together

✓ **Word Choice** When you write a **class story**, choose interesting words that are just right! Don't use the same word again and again.

Ms. Soto's class wrote about their town. Later, they changed **big** to a clearer word.

Revised Draft

Our town has a big parade.

Funny clowns wear ~~big~~ <u>tall</u> hats.

Revising Checklist

 Does our story have interesting details?

 Did we use nouns that are exact?

 Did we use adjectives to tell about size or shape?

Find words in Ms. Soto's class story that help you picture the parade. Then revise your class story. Use the Checklist.

Final Copy

Our Town Parade

Our town has a big parade.

Funny clowns wear tall hats.

A fire truck blasts its

horn. Horses prance

down wide streets.

✓ WORDS TO KNOW
HIGH-FREQUENCY WORDS

many
friend
full
pull
hold
good

Vocabulary Reader

Context Cards

Words to Know

● **Read each Context Card.**

● **Use a blue word to tell about something you did.**

1

many

There are many cars on the street.

2

friend

She likes to ride the bus with her friend.

3 full

This train is always full of people.

4 pull

He can pull his pet in the wagon.

5 hold

She can hold up her hand to get a taxi.

6 good

The ferry is a good way to see the city.

Background

✓ **WORDS TO KNOW** **All Aboard!**

1. **Many** people like train rides.

2. It is fun to sit with a **friend**.

3. There is a shelf to **hold** your bag.

4. Sometimes all the seats are **full**.

5. Everyone will have a **good** time!

6. The conductor will **pull** the whistle cord.

A Train Ride

train   conductor   bags   seats

Comprehension

✓ **TARGET SKILL** Story Structure

A story has different parts. The **characters** are the people and animals in a story. The **setting** is when and where a story takes place. The **plot** is the order of story events. It tells what problem the characters have and how they solve it.

As you read **Gus Takes the Train**, use a story map to describe who is in the story, where they are, and what they do.

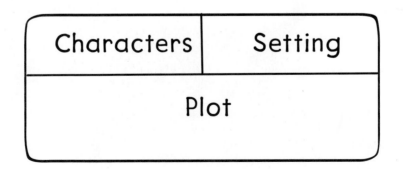

Characters	Setting
Plot	

✔ **WORDS TO KNOW**

many	pull
friend	hold
full	good

✔ **TARGET SKILL**

Story Structure Tell the setting, characters, and events in a story.

✔ **TARGET STRATEGY**

Analyze/Evaluate Tell how you feel about the text, and why.

GENRE

A **fantasy** is a story that could not happen in real life.

Meet the Author and Illustrator

Russell Benfanti

If you like Russell Benfanti's colorful artwork, then visit a toy store. There you will find board games, toy packages, and computer games that Mr. Benfanti designed. "I love what I do!" he says.

Gus Takes the Train

written and illustrated by Russell Benfanti

Essential Question
How does the setting make a story interesting?

Gus has to run to get the train.
He has a big bag to pull.

Run, Gus, run!

Gus cannot pull up his bag.
The conductor can help him.

The train is full.
Gus can see many kids.

Gus sat.

His big bag can go up here.

Gus met a friend!
Peg and Gus sing and play.

Peg can hold the cups for Gus.
They are too full!

Peg and Gus have a sip.
It is good!

Gus can see a lot.

A funny bug is on the window!

We are here!
Gus had fun on the train.

Your Turn

Let's Take a Trip

Make Trading Cards Work with a group to make cards that show different ways people travel. Then take turns choosing a card. Tell where you would go and what you would see on your trip. SMALL GROUP

Turn and Talk — A Fun Ride

Tell the story to a partner. Tell it the way Peg would tell it. Then tell why you think Gus and Peg had fun on the train. STORY STRUCTURE

City Zoo

Connect to Social Studies

✔ **WORDS TO KNOW**

many	pull
friend	hold
full	good

GENRE

Informational text gives facts about a topic. What is the topic of the selection?

TEXT FOCUS

A **map** is a drawing of a place. A **key** shows what pictures on the map mean. What does each picture in the key on page 127 mean?

City Zoo

Welcome to the City Zoo! The zoo is full of many interesting animals. See if you can find all the animals on the map.

Key

tiger

elephant

polar bear

giraffe

We hope you have a good time at the zoo.

- Come with your family and a friend.

- Hold on to your ticket.

- Have some snacks.

- Pull a wagon.

- Take pictures.

Making Connections

Text to Self

Write a Description Write to tell your classmates about a time you went on a trip. Tell them what you saw and did.

Text to Text

Compare Stories Think about the selections. Tell which is make-believe. Which is true? How do you know?

Text to World

Connect to Social Studies Imagine that you are traveling to study animals. Where would you go? Find that place on a map or globe.

Grammar

Read Together

Adjectives Some **adjectives** describe people, animals, places, or things by telling their color or how many.

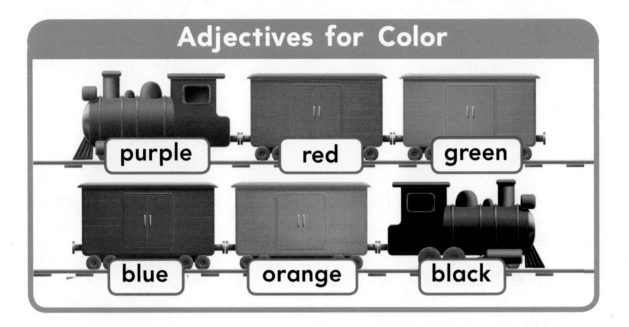

Adjectives for Color

purple red green

blue orange black

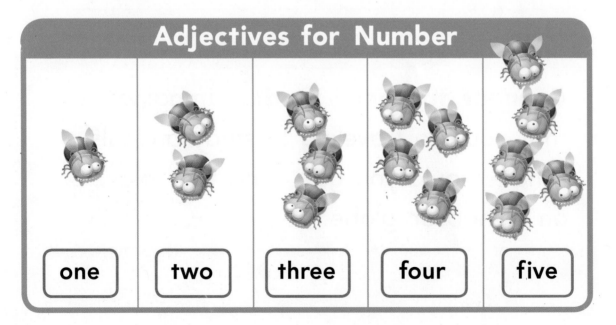

Adjectives for Number

one two three four five

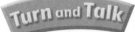

Turn and Talk

Use one number adjective and one color adjective to describe each picture. Talk with your partner about how adjectives help you tell how things look.

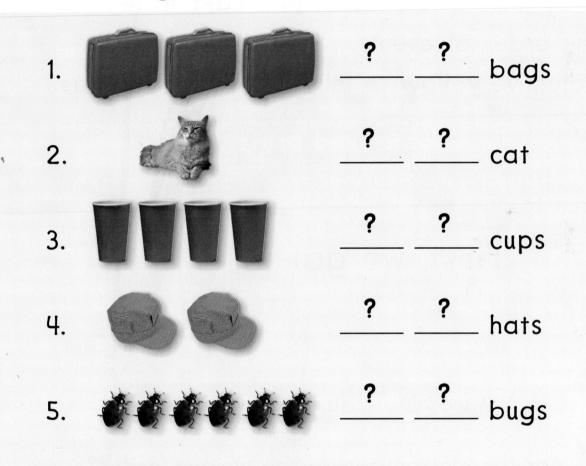

1. **?** ____ **?** ____ bags

2. **?** ____ **?** ____ cat

3. **?** ____ **?** ____ cups

4. **?** ____ **?** ____ hats

5. **?** ____ **?** ____ bugs

Grammar in Writing

When you revise your writing, look for places where you can add some adjectives.

Writing About Us

Read Together

☑ Ideas When you write a **class story**, use adjectives to describe things clearly.

Mr. Tam's class wrote about a bus trip. They used **First, Next,** and **Last** to tell the order of events. Then they added the adjective **yellow** to tell more about the bus.

Revised Draft

First, we got on a ^ bus.

yellow

Revising Checklist

 Are the story events in the correct order?

 Did we use words like **first, next,** and **last** to show the order?

 Could we tell more by adding adjectives?

Read the class story. Find adjectives.
Find words that tell order. Now help revise
your class story. Use the Checklist.

Final Copy

A City Bus Ride

Our class took a bus trip.

First, we got on a yellow bus.

Next, we sang two songs.

Last, we saw tall
buildings and
long trains.

Read the next two stories. Then tell the main idea of each story.

A Pet for Tim

My dad said, "Tim, you can get a pet."

My friends have pets I like.

Dan has Mac the dog.

Mac likes to run and play.

A dog is a fun pet.

Jed has Bev the bird.

It can sing and speak.

It says funny things.

Bev stays in.

Mel has Dot the cat.

All she does is stay in and nap!

I want a pet that can go out.

Fun at the Zoo

Pam and Mom go to the zoo.

First, they go to see the cubs.

The cubs hop in the mud.

They make a big mess!

Next, they see the big cats.

The big cats nap in the sun.

Last, Pam and Mom go to see the funny seals.

The man chooses Pam to help him.

Pam helps him with the fish.

Pam and Mom have fun at the zoo!

Unit 1 Wrap-Up

Read Together

The Big  Idea

Neighborhood Map

Make a picture map of your neighborhood. Show where people live, work, and play. Draw pictures of buildings, roads, and parks. Write a title that tells about your map.

Listening and Speaking

A Helper Is a Good Neighbor

Think of the people you see at home and in school. Tell a story about a time when one of those people helped you.

136

Words to Know

Unit 1 High-Frequency Words

1 What Is a Pal?
play
be
and
help
with
you

2 The Storm
he
look
have
for
too
what

3 Curious George at School
sing
do
they
find
no
funny

4 Lucia's Neighborhood
my
here
who
all
does
me

5 Gus Takes the Train
many
friend
full
pull
hold
good

Glossary

B

bed

A **bed** is a kind of furniture for sleeping. I sleep in my **bed**.

book

A **book** is a group of pages with words on them. **Frog and Toad** is my favorite **book**.

C

car

A **car** is a machine with four wheels. We go in a **car** to visit my grandparents.

come

To **come** means to move toward something. Maria called the puppy to **come** to her.

conductor

The **conductor** is the person in charge of a train. The train **conductor** watched the tracks closely.

curious

To be **curious** is to want to learn. Alan was **curious** about dinosaurs.

F

firefighter's

A **firefighter** is someone who puts out fires. A **firefighter's** job can be dangerous.

fun

To have **fun** is to have a good time. The children had **fun** playing tag.

G

George
George is a boy's name. My dad's name is **George**.

goal
A **goal** is a score in a game. Anita kicked the ball and made a **goal**.

H

hi
The word **hi** means hello. I say **hi** when I see someone I know.

home
A **home** is a place where people or animals live. There are six people living in my **home**.

J

job
A **job** is work for people to do. Uncle Ned has a **job** in a store.

K

kids

Kid is another word for child. My uncle tells funny stories about when he and my dad were **kids**.

L

librarian

A **librarian** works in a place where many books are kept. The **librarian** helped me find the book I was looking for.

Lucia

Lucia is a girl's name. My sister's name is **Lucia**.

M

mess

A **mess** is something that is not neat. My sister's room is a **mess!**

N

neighborhood

A **neighborhood** is a part of a city or town. Jim walks to the store in his **neighborhood**.

P

paints

Paints are liquids with colors in them. Dip the big brushes into the **paints**.

pal

A **pal** is a friend. Benny is my best **pal**.

pants

People wear **pants** over their legs. Lucy's **pants** have two big pockets.

pet

A **pet** is an animal who lives with you. My cat Sam is the best **pet** ever!

plant

A **plant** is anything alive that is not a person or an animal. We have a **plant** with big green leaves in our kitchen.

Pop

Pop is one name for a grandfather. I call my mother's father **Pop**.

S

school

A **school** is a place where students learn from teachers. I learn to read at **school**.

storm

A **storm** is strong wind or snow. Lots of rain fell during the **storm**.

street

A **street** is a road in a city or a town. We live on a very busy **street**.

T

takes

The word **takes** can mean to travel by. Mia **takes** the bus to school.

this

This means something that is near you. **This** is the book I'm taking home.

train

A **train** is a group of railroad cars. This summer my family is going on a **train** ride.

W

wet
Wet means covered with liquid. Juan got **wet** when he went out in the rain.

what
The word **what** is used to ask questions. **What** did you eat for breakfast?

window
A **window** is an open place in a wall. Sasha opened the **window.**

Acknowledgments

"Damon & Blue" from *My Man Blue* by Nikki Grimes. Copyright © 1999 by Nikki Grimes. Reprinted by permission of Dial Books for Young Readers, a division of Penguin Young Readers Group, a member of Penguin Group (USA) Inc., 345 Hudson Street, New York, NY 10014 and Curtis Brown, Ltd.

"Jambo" from *Nightfeathers* by Sundaira Morninghouse. Copyright © 1989 by Sundaira Morninghouse. Reprinted by permission of Open Hand Publishing, LLC (www.openhand.com).

"Wait for Me" by Sarah Wilson from *June Is a Tune That Jumps on a Stair*. Copyright © 1992 by Sarah Wilson. Reprinted by permission of the author.

Curious George's®Day at School, text by Houghton Mifflin Harcourt and illustrated by H.A. Rey and Margaret Rey. Text copyright © 2010 by Houghton Mifflin Harcourt Publishing Company. Illustrations copyright © 2010 by H.A. Rey and Margaret Rey. Reprinted by permission of Houghton Mifflin Harcourt Publishing Company. All rights reserved.

The character, Curious George®, including without limitation the character's name and the character's likenesses, are registered trademarks of Houghton Mifflin Harcourt Publishing Company. Curious George logo is a tradmark of Houghton Mifflin Harcourt Publishing Company. Add to front or back cover and/or spine of every book and advertisements: Curious George® .

Credits

Photo Credits

Placement Key: (t) top; (b) bottom; (l) left; (r) right; (c) center; (bkgd) background; (frgd) foreground; (i) inset.

8a HMH/Ken Karp; **8b** HMH/Ken Karp; (i) ©Image Source/Corbis; **9** (tc) (c)Image Source/Corbis; **10** (t) (c)Ariel Skelley/Corbis; **10** (b) (c)Ariel Skelley/Corbis; **11** (tl) (c)Bob Krist/Corbis; **11** (tr) (c)Ariel Skelley/Corbis; **11** (bl) (c) Dirk Anschutz/Stone/Getty Images; **11** (br) (c) Paul Austring Photography/First Light/Getty Images; **13** (c) Rommel/Masterfile; **14-33** (c) HMH/Nina Crews; **26-27** (c)Heide Benser/zefa/Corbis; **28-29** (c)Colin Hogan/Alamy; **30** (tl) (c) Ryan McVay/Photodisc/Alamy; **30** (tr) (c)SW Productions/Photodisc/Getty Images; **30** (bl) (c) Juniors Bildarchiv/Alamy; (br) (c)Gay Bumgarner/Photographer's Choice/Getty Images; **31** (tl) (c)Julian Winslow/Corbis; **31** (cl) (c)CMCD/PhotoDisc; **31** (bl) (c)Rachel Watson/Stone/Getty Images; **31** (tr) (c)Masterfile; **31** (cr) Photospin; **34** (t) (c)Amy Etra/PhotoEdit; **34** (b) (c)Spencer Grant/PhotoEdit; **35** (tl) (c)Sascha Pflaeging/Riser/Getty Images; **35** (bl) (c)Richard Hutchings/PhotoEdit; **35** (br) (c)Jupiter Images/Comstock Images/Alamy; **35** (tr) (c)Thomas Barwick/Riser/Getty Images; **36** (b) (c) Masterfile; **38** (c)Courtesy of Raul Colon; **50-51** (c)Douglas Keister/Corbis; **52** (bg) (c)Photodisc/Don Farrall, Lightworks Studio; **52** (tr) (c)Spencer Grant/PhotoEdit; **52** (br) (c)Authors Image/Alamy; **52** (bl) (c)Matthias Engelien/Alamy; **52** (tl) (c)David Young-Wolff/PhotoEdit; **53** (b) (c)Glow Images/Alamy; **55** (bl) (c)Patrick Bennett/Corbis; **55** (tr) Corbis;